DOG BREEDS

Pugs

by Anne Wendorff

Consultant:
Michael Leuthner, D.V.M.
PetCare Clinic, Madison, Wisc.

BLASTOFF! READERS
4

BELLWETHER MEDIA · MINNEAPOLIS, MN

Note to Librarians, Teachers, and Parents:

Blastoff! Readers are carefully developed by literacy experts and combine standards-based content with developmentally appropriate text.

Level 1 provides the most support through repetition of high-frequency words, light text, predictable sentence patterns, and strong visual support.

Level 2 offers early readers a bit more challenge through varied simple sentences, increased text load, and less repetition of high-frequency words.

Level 3 advances early-fluent readers toward fluency through increased text and concept load, less reliance on visuals, longer sentences, and more literary language.

Level 4 builds reading stamina by providing more text per page, increased use of punctuation, greater variation in sentence patterns, and increasingly challenging vocabulary.

Level 5 encourages children to move from "learning to read" to "reading to learn" by providing even more text, varied writing styles, and less familiar topics.

Whichever book is right for your reader, Blastoff! Readers are the perfect books to build confidence and encourage a love of reading that will last a lifetime!

This edition first published in 2010 by Bellwether Media, Inc.

No part of this publication may be reproduced in whole or in part without written permission of the publisher. For information regarding permission, write to Bellwether Media, Inc., Attention: Permissions Department, 5357 Penn Avenue South, Minneapolis, MN 55419.

Library of Congress Cataloging-in-Publication Data
Wendorff, Anne.
Pugs / by Anne Wendorff.
   p. cm. – (Blastoff! Readers dog breeds)
Includes bibliographical references and index.
Summary: "Simple text and full-color photography introduce beginning readers to the characteristics of the dog breed Pugs. Developed by literacy experts for students in kindergarten through third grade"–Provided by publisher.
ISBN 978-1-60014-301-4 (hardcover : alk. paper)
1. Pug–Juvenile literature. I. Title.
SF429.P9W46 2010
636.76–dc22

                        2009037210

Printed in the United States of America, North Mankato, MN.
010110   1149

Contents

What Are Pugs?   4

History of Pugs   10

Pugs Today   14

Glossary   22

To Learn More   23

Index   24

What Are Pugs?

Pugs are small **companion dogs**. They are friendly and easy-going. They have large, deep wrinkles around their heads and necks. Their tails curl back toward their bodies.

Pugs have square bodies. They weigh between 13 and 20 pounds (6 and 9 kilograms). They are 10 to 14 inches (25 to 35 centimeters) tall.

! **fun fact**

Pugs are often described as being *multum in parvo*. It means a lot of dog in a small space.

Pugs have short hair and **shed** a lot. Almost every Pug has black or **fawn** hair. All Pugs have black **muzzles**. Their muzzles are also called their masks. Pugs are known for having flat muzzles and small, short noses. Their muzzles are often covered in moles and wrinkles!

Their small, flat noses make it hard for Pugs to breathe. Pugs have trouble breathing when they lie down. This is why Pugs snore and **wheeze** in their sleep.

Pugs cannot exercise for very long.
They get tired quickly and need to rest.

History of Pugs

Pugs are a very old **breed** of dog. Chinese emperors and Tibetan monks kept Pugs as pets over 2,000 years ago. When English soldiers invaded Asia, they brought Pugs back to Europe. Pugs became a favorite pet for royal families in Holland, England, and France.

Pugs were brought to America to be pets. In America, the **American Kennel Club (AKC)** keeps track of all **purebred** dog breeds.

They also hold dog shows. The American Kennel Club decided Pugs were an official breed in 1885.

Pugs Today

Pugs belong to the **toy group** of dog breeds. Members of the toy group are small dogs. These dogs compete against each other in dog shows, obedience events, and **agility**. In dog shows, judges examine the dogs and score the way they look and act. Pugs do well in dog shows because they are easy to train.

In obedience events, Pugs must follow directions from their owners.

Owners tell their dogs to sit, follow, retrieve, drop, and more. Judges score how well the dogs respond to the commands. Dogs that perform well have the best chance at winning.

In agility, Pugs jump through hoops, run around poles, and run through tunnels.

Judges score how well the dogs move through the agility course. They also measure their time.

Pugs can be playful or calm. They can **adapt** to different homes and can be trained to perform tricks.

Pugs like to play with children and adults. They are very loyal pets. They are good companion dogs because they are friendly and eager to please!

Glossary

adapt—to change behavior based on surroundings

agility—a sport where dogs run through a series of obstacles

American Kennel Club (AKC)—a group that monitors and promotes purebred dogs

breed—a type of dog

companion dogs—dogs that provide friendship to people

fawn—a light tan and white color

muzzle—the nose, jaws, and mouth of an animal

purebred—a dog whose mother and father were the same breed

shed—to lose hair

toy group—a group of small dogs

wheeze—to breathe with a whistling sound

To Learn More

AT THE LIBRARY

Haskins Houran, Lori. *Pug: What a Mug*. New York, N.Y.: Bearport Publishing Co., 2009.

Heinrichs Gray, Susan. *Pugs*. Mankato, Minn.: The Child's World, 2007.

Hubbard, Woodleigh. *For the Love of a Pug*. New York, N.Y.: Penguin Young Reader Group, 2003.

ON THE WEB

Learning more about Pugs is as easy as 1, 2, 3.

1. Go to www.factsurfer.com.

2. Enter "Pugs" into the search box.

3. Click the "Surf" button and you will see a list of related Web sites.

With factsurfer.com, finding more information is just a click away.

Index

1885, 13
adapting, 20
agility, 14, 18, 19
America, 12
American Kennel Club
    (AKC), 12, 13
Asia, 10
breathing, 8
breed, 10, 12, 13, 14,
    15
Chihuahuas, 15
Chinese emperors, 10
companion dogs, 4, 21
dog shows, 13, 14
England, 10
English soldiers, 10
Europe, 10
exercise, 9
fawn, 7
France, 10
hair, 6, 7
height, 5

Holland, 10
judges, 14, 17, 19
muzzles, 7
obedience events, 14, 16
Poodles, 15
purebred breed, 12
shedding, 7
terriers, 15
Tibetan monks, 10
toy group, 14, 15
weight, 5
wheezing, 8

The images in this book are reproduced through the courtesy of: Helen E. Grose, front cover; Minden Pictures, p. 4; Daniel Hughes, p. 5; Juniors Bildarchiv, pp. 6-7, 9, 10-11; Luca Bertolli, p. 7; J. Harrison/Kimballstock, p. 8; Jessica Miller, p. 12; Juan Martinez, p. 13; Nicky Dronoff-Guthrie, pp. 14-15, 18, 19; Klein-Hubert/Kimballstock, p. 16; Stan Kujawa, p. 17; Bob Scoverski, p. 20; Sarah M. Golonka, p. 21.